Gregory's Pita Pocket
Full of Simple Greek Recipes

By

Gregory Evangelos Zotos, MA ED
Γρηγορη

Sylvia-
Happy
Cooking!!

PublishAmerica
Baltimore

First printing

ISBN: 1-4137-1207-X
PUBLISHED BY PUBLISHAMERICA, LLLP
www.publishamerica.com
Baltimore

Printed in the United States of America

I would like to dedicate this book to my magnificent mother Cathy Zotos, who has enhanced my life by the glow of her love. To my late father Evangelos Zotos and my late sister Connie Zotos, who will always be angels in my heart. In addition, to my Yia Yia and Papou (Grandmother and Grandfather) whose inspiration and love have been so valuable to my life.

Acknowledgments

I would like to acknowledge Rebecca Embree of PublishAmerica for giving my book a chance to be published. I thank her from the bottom of my heart.

Author's Note

This book allows you prepare and taste the mouth-watering old recipes that were prepared in the old (Horia) villages in Greece. I have put together a wonderful collection of recipes that I have made very simple and easy to prepare. The taste of Greece will await the purchaser of this book.

It is very difficult to find a Greek cookbook that captures the old village recipes that have that outstanding taste one can get only by the preparation in the old village. I have captured this in my recipe book. I would like to offer others the opportunity to purchase my fine book and be able to experience simple, great, Greek recipes.

I have included a page labeled "cooking instructions" after every recipe. This page is a very effective tool for everyone to utilize. When you are cooking and you perhaps do not want the recipe as spicey the next time you make it, you may jot this type of note down under the cooking instructions. This way the next time you cook it, you will remember that helpful hint.

Oven temperatures vary. Another helpful cooking note may be if a recipe got done earlier than stated, your oven temperature is a little different. Please note this in the cooking instructions for future use.

Avgolemono Soup (Chicken Egg Lemon Soup)

- 2 eggs
- 1 lemon, squeezed
- 1 whole chicken
- 2 tablespoons dill
- 1 cup rice or orzo
- 2 onions, chopped
- salt
- pepper

Place the chicken in a large pot and fill with water until the chicken is fully covered. Bring to a boil. Now add the onion and salt and pepper to taste. Add the dill. When the chicken comes to a boil, add the rice or orzo to the pot and let it boil. When the rice or orzo is cooked, add the egg lemon mix. Beat the eggs and add the lemon juice and stock from soup alternately. Beat well.

COOKING NOTES:

Fakkes (Lentil Soup)

- 1 full pound of lentils
- 4-5 cloves of garlic
- salt
- 1 carrot
- 1 stalk celery
- pepper
- 1 cup extra virgin olive oil
- 1 large onion, chopped
- 1 8 oz. can tomato sauce
- 1 bay leaf

Wash the lentils in cold water. Place the lentils in a pot with enough water to cover them. Boil for 10 minutes. Add the rest of the ingredients. Slowly simmer for about an hour or until done.

COOKING NOTES:

Tzatziki

- 2 teaspoons extra virgin olive oil
- 1¼ cup plain yogurt
- 1 large cucumber, finely chopped
- 3 cloves garlic, minced
- 4 green onions, chopped
- ¾ teaspoon vinegar
- 1¼ teaspoon dill, chopped

Begin by peeling the cucumber and removing the seeds. Cut into small chunks and chop finely.

Mix garlic, chopped cucumber chunks, green onions, extra virgin olive oil, vinegar, and dill. Mix in the yogurt.

Put in the refrigerator, cover for 2 ¼ hours. Serve with Greek bread, as an appetizer, or plain.

COOKING NOTES:

Greek Salad

- 1 head lettuce
- 2¼ sliced tomatoes
- 1 sliced cucumber
- 1 sliced green or red pepper
- 25 Kalamata Greek olives
- 1 sliced onion
- salt, pepper, oregano
- 1 cup imported Greek feta cheese

Cut or tear lettuce up and put in a big salad bowl or dish.

Add cucumbers, tomatoes, onions, green peppers, imported Greek feta cheese, and Kalamata olives.

Dressing is the traditional extra virgin olive oil and vinegar. Pour all over the salad. Mix carefully and serve right away for crisp, traditional Greek taste.

COOKING NOTES:

Koulourakia Cookies

- 3 cups white flour
- 1 teaspoon baking powder
- 1 cup real butter
- ½ cup pure sugar
- 2 large eggs
- 1 teaspoon metaxa
- 1 tablespoon orange juice
- ¾ cup of sesame seeds

Sift dry ingredients very well. Beat eggs and save 1 yolk for brushing over the koulourakia in the pan. Add the butter mixture, beating very well. (Mix butter and sugar to a whipped, fluffy texture.) Add the eggs to this mixture. Add to dry ingredients to create a soft dough and add metaxa and orange juice. Knead softly until smooth. Shape pieces of dough into thick pencil shapes. Roll dough and twist, to create figure eights.

Put on greased baking sheets and glaze with the saved beaten egg yolk. Roll onto the sesame seeds to coat. Bake in oven at 375 degrees for 12-17 minutes or until golden brown. Cool and store in an airtight container.

COOKING NOTES:

Taramosalata Greek Caviar

- 4 ounces Tarama
- 1 cup extra virgin olive oil
- 1 small onion, chopped fine
- 1 pound boiled potatoes
- 3 fresh-squeezed lemons

Smash the onions, potatoes and tarama together. Smash until it becomes very silky and rich. Now add the extra virgin olive oil and the fresh-squeezed lemon juice together in little amounts while smashing. When serving, place Kalamata olives around the outer rim of the dish for appearance and for a true Greek taste.

COOKING NOTES:

Kalamari (Fried Squid)

- 3 pounds squid
- extra virgin olive oil
- 5 lemons
- flour to coat the squid
- 1 cup finely grated onions
- Greek sea salt or regular salt

Combine the salt with the flour. Clean the squid and put the squid in the flour to coat it. Fry the squid in hot olive oil. Sprinkle onions over the squid and season with lemon to your taste.

COOKING NOTES:

Saganaki Greek Flaming Cheese

- 1 pound kasseri cheese
- 1 lemon, cut in half
- 1 cup real butter
- flaming brandy
- matches

Slice 1-inch thick slices of kasseri. Warm the butter in a frying pan and place the cheese in the pan. When the cheese begins to brown, pour the flaming brandy over the cheese for the flame. Light the match and put the flame over the cheese. The cheese will start on fire. Squeeze the lemon over the flames. This will put out the fire and season the cheese. Cut and enjoy over Greek bread.

Caution: be very careful when utilizing the matches, flames, etc.

COOKING NOTES:

Spanakopita (Spinach Pie)

- 2 pounds fresh spinach
- 1 pound sliced green onions
- 1 cup extra virgin olive oil
- ¼ cup dill
- 2 thinly sliced leeks
- 4 eggs
- 1 pound Greek filo
- Greek sea salt or regular salt
- fresh ground pepper
- 1 pound Greek imported feta cheese

Wash the spinach and boil it. Pour spinach in a strainer and strain. Then tear up the spinach in little pieces. Brown the green onions and the leek in a pot using half the olive oil. Turn the burner off and add the eggs, dill, spinach, salt, and pepper. Oil a sheet pan and open the filo sheets across the pan, about 40% of the sheets.

Put the spinach combination over the filo and then place the remaining filo sheets over the spinach. Oil the top and bake in medium (350 degree) oven for about 1 hour.

COOKING NOTES:

Greek Seafood Gyro

- 4 full pita bread, Greek
- 1 sea bass fish filet, medium size, cooked and chopped
- 1 large tomato, cut up
- ¼ head of lettuce
- 3 garlic cloves, chopped
- ¾ cup chopped onions
- ¼ pound Greek feta cheese
- ¼ pound Greek kasseri
- ¼ teaspoon black pepper, ground
- ¾ cup yogurt

Put all ingredients in a big mixing bowl and mix all the ingredients together by mashing and mixing them. Scoop out and put into pita bread. You will enjoy this as a lunch or dinner entrée.

COOKING NOTES:

Greek Corn on the Cob

- ¼ cup oregano
- ½ cup melted butter
- ¼ cup ground pepper
- ½ cup minced garlic
- 5 corns on the cob

Peel off the green covering over the corn on the cob. Put in a pan of boiling water and salt (about 3 pinches) for 10 minutes. In a mixing bowl mix the rest of the ingredients very well so all the ingredients are fully mixed. Put in the boiling pan of water and cook for another 4 minutes.

COOKING NOTES:

Protokalla Tea (Orange Tea)

- 4 oranges
- 1 bunch Greek tea stems with leaves
- 3 teaspoons sugar (optional)

Squeeze the oranges into orange juice and put into a glass. Boil the Greek tea stems with leaves for 6 minutes in a pan of boiling water. Strain. Pour the boiling water into a cup. Add the fresh-squeezed orange juice into the cup. This can also be served cold. After the water has boiled for 6 minutes, strain. Then let sit for 15 minutes to cool. Then chill. Serve with the fresh-squeezed orange juice cold.

COOKING NOTES:

Greek Cod Fish

- 2 medium cod fish fillets
- 1 cup fresh diced tomatoes
- 6 ounces extra virgin olive oil
- ¼ cup minced garlic
- ¼ cup oregano
- 3 pinches sea salt
- 3 pinches fresh ground pepper
- ½ cup Greek white wine
- 2 finely chopped onions

Put the fish in a butter or an oiled casserole dish. Mix all ingredients together. Put all ingredients over the fish and around the fish. Bake at 350 degrees for 40 minutes for the Greek well-done taste.

COOKING NOTES:

Greek Salmon

- 1½ pound very fresh salmon fillet
- ¼ cup extra virgin olive oil
- ¼ cup fresh dill weed
- 4 lemons
- ¼ cup Greek feta cheese
- ¼ cup Greek kasseri cheese

Rinse salmon very, very well and place in a buttered or oiled casserole pan, skin side down. Mix all ingredients together and squeeze the lemons into the mixed ingredients. Put the mixed ingredients over the salmon and around the salmon in the pan. Broil the salmon until opaque in center. This is about 7 minutes for a ¾-inch salmon.

COOKING NOTES:

Greek Pasta Orzo Salad

- ¼ cup oregano
- ¼ cup Greek feta cheese
- ¼ cup Greek kasseri cheese
- 1¼ cup orzo
- ¼ cup lettuce
- ¼ cup Greek olives, black
- 3 pinches sea salt
- 6 pinches black pepper
- 1/3 cup extra virgin olive oil
- 1/8 cup of vinegar

Orzo should be boiled for 7 minutes in a boiling pan. Drain the orzo and place in a large bowl. Add each ingredient separately to the salad. Mix gently and serve.

COOKING NOTES:

Greek Cheesecake Snacks

- 1/3 cup sugar
- ¼ teaspoon vanilla
- 3 eggs
- 16 ounces any soft Greek cheese
- 10 Greek wafers

Mix the sugar, vanilla, eggs, and soft Greek cheese. Put over the wafers and put the wafers on an oiled or buttered cookie sheet. Bake for 15 minutes in a preheated 350-degree oven. Remove and enjoy.

COOKING NOTES:

Fried Kasseri Cheese Snacks

- ¾ pound Greek kasseri cheese
- ¼ cup milk
- ¾ cup buttermilk baking mix
- 1 egg
- ¾ cup extra virgin olive oil

Heat olive oil in a pan about 9 inches tall until it comes to a boil. Beat the egg, milk, and buttermilk baking mix until a doughy mix appears. Then cut the Greek kasseri cheese into cubes and put the dough around a cube. Place the cube in the boiling olive oil for 2 minutes and remove. Let cool and enjoy.

COOKING NOTES:

Greek Jelly Slices

- ½ cup Greek jelly or jam
- ½ cup soft butter
- ½ cup brown sugar
- ½ cup chopped pecans
- 8 slices Greek bread

Heat oven to 445 degrees. Spread butter over the slices of Greek bread. Spread the Greek jelly or jam over the butter. Pinch the brown sugar over the jam until a light coat appears. Pinch the chopped pecans over the brown sugar until a coating appears. Bake on a cookie sheet for 6 minutes or until you see small bubbles forming on top. Remove, cool and enjoy.

COOKING NOTES:

Ouzo Apple Juice

- ¼ cup Greek ouzo
- 2 quarts fresh apple cider
- ¼ cup sugar

Mix the Greek ouzo, fresh apple cider, and sugar in a pitcher. Chill and serve. This will be the light of the party.

COOKING NOTES:

Greek Fried Eggs

- 3 eggs
- 4 tablespoons extra virgin olive oil
- 5 slices Greek kefalotyri cheese
- 2 pinches black pepper

Put the 4 tablespoons of extra virgin olive oil in a frying pan and heat until it bubbles. Add eggs. Let eggs cook until done. Put the slices of kefalotyri over the eggs. Cover the pan; leave until cheese has melted. Enjoy.

COOKING NOTES:

Greek Candy Sesame Seed

- ¼ cup water
- 1/8 cup sugar
- ¾ cup pure Greek honey
- 4 cups sesame seeds

Mix all the ingredients together in a pan. Place pan on stove on medium heat and stir constantly. When the liquid is a tan color, turn off heat. Spread in an oiled or buttered cookie sheet pan. Let set for15 minutes. Break off pieces and serve.

COOKING NOTES:

Greek Coffee

- 2 teaspoons any brand of Greek coffee
- ¾ teaspoon sugar
- ½ cup water

Put coffee, sugar and water in a tall narrow pan. Put on stove and allow to come to a boil. Slowly pour into a coffee cup or a small 2-inch Greek coffee cup. Add more sugar if desired.

COOKING NOTES:

Greek Macaroni

- 1 cup grated Greek feta cheese
- ½ cup butter
- 16 ounces Greek macaroni (American macaroni may be substituted)

Cook the macaroni for 6 to 8 minutes in boiling water with a pinch of salt. Melt butter in a small pan. In a big dish put ¼ of the drained macaroni. Pour a little butter and sprinkle some Greek feta cheese, repeat for the remaining quarters. Enjoy!

COOKING NOTES:

Greek Artichoke Omelet

- 6 beaten eggs
- 6 tablespoons extra virgin olive oil
- ¼ cup chopped onions
- ¼ cup oregano
- 12 ounces artichoke hearts
- 3 cloves garlic or minced garlic

Pour the extra virgin olive oil in a pan and heat until small bubbles appear. Then add all the other ingredients. Cook until eggs are set, at a low heat setting.

COOKING NOTES:

Greek Kasseri Cheese Pita Sandwich

- 5 tablespoons extra virgin olive oil
- 5 tablespoons vinegar
- 6 slices Greek kasseri cheese
- 1¼ cup shredded lettuce
- 1 medium tomato, diced
- ½ cup diced cucumber
- 4 tablespoons chopped peppers
- 2 Greek pita breads

Combine the ingredients and hand mix well except for the kasseri cheese. Place the mixed ingredients in a pita bread and then put 3 slices of Greek kasseri cheese over the ingredients. Enjoy as a snack, lunch or dinner.

COOKING NOTES:

Horiatiki Salata (Village Salad)

- 1 cup Kalamata Greek olives
- 1 cup beets
- 1 cucumber, sliced
- 3 tomatoes, sliced
- 1 cup Greek feta cheese
- 1 small head lettuce
- ¾ cup extra virgin olive oil
- ½ cup wine vinegar
- ½ cup oregano

Tear the lettuce up and put into a bowl. Place the Kalamata Greek olives on top of the lettuce. Then place the slices of onions on top of the olives. Then place the cucumber slices on top of the onions. Place the beets on top of the cumber slices. Place the Greek feta cheese on top of the beets. Sprinkle the oregano over the whole salad. Also add the oil and the vinegar.

If you put everything in the order suggested, it will give the salad a beautiful color and a true Greek taste. Enjoy.

COOKING NOTES:

Greek Yogurt Cucumber Appetizer

- ¼ cup dill weed
- 2 cucumbers
- 1 cup yogurt
- 1 large onion, sliced
- 2 fresh lemons
- ¼ cup oregano

Slice the cucumbers in medium thickness and layer on a flat dish. Place the sliced onions on top of the cucumbers. Spread the yogurt evenly over all the onions and cucumbers. Squeeze the lemons over the yogurt. Sprinkle the dill weed and oregano over the whole appetizer.

COOKING NOTES:

Flaming Sausage

- 1 long sausage sliced into 10 slices
- ¼ cup oregano
- 1 teaspoon pepper
- 1 teaspoon salt
- ¼ cup extra virgin olive oil
- 1/8 cup Virginia dare flaming brandy
- 1 lemon

Put the olive oil in an all-steel frying pan. Cook the sausage in the olive oil. When the sausage begins to brown, turn the heat off. Sprinkle the salt, pepper, and oregano over the sausage. CAREFULLY pour the Virginia dare flaming brandy over the sausage and light with a match. The sausage will have a flame. Leave for 10 seconds and squeeze the lemon over the flames. This will make the flames go out and give it taste.

COOKING NOTES:

Old Traditional Greek Village Salad

- 1 large onion, sliced into half slices
- 3 tomatoes, sliced into half slices
- ¾ cup extra virgin olive oil
- ¾ cup crumbled Greek feta cheese
- ¼ cup black pepper
- ¼ cup salt
- ¾ cup oregano

The old traditional village salad is made by just combining all the ingredients and mixing them together. This is a very old traditional village salad.

COOKING NOTES:

Greek Lemon Rice Soup (Avyolemono Soopa)

- 1 cup rice
- ½ cup chopped onions
- ½ cup lemon juice
- 3 eggs
- 1 cup water
- 3 cans chicken broth
- white meat from one chicken
- salt to taste
- pepper to taste

Boil the rice, chicken, chicken broth, salt, pepper, and onions until done. Beat the egss well. Add alternately chicken broth and lemon to egg mixture. Pour into pan with chicken. Turn heat off and let sit for a few minutes to cool a little bit.

COOKING NOTES:

Greek Hamburgers (Beef Stekee)

- ¼ cup extra virgin olive oil
- 1 package hamburger buns
- 1¼ pound ground beef
- 1 tablespoon lemon juice
- 1/4 teaspoon salt
- ¼ teaspoon pepper
- ¾ cup crumbled Greek feta cheese
- 12 Greek Kalamata olives, remove pits
- 1/8 cup dill weed
- 2 cups yogurt
- 2 sliced tomatoes
- 1 cucumber, sliced

Put together all the ingredients in a large mixing bowl except for the yogurt, tomatoes, and cucumbers, which will be used for garnishing. Mix by hand so all the ingredients are mixed well. Form into hamburgers.

Cook on a grill or broil in the oven on a greased cookie sheet for about 10 minutes on each side or until brown. Place in hamburger bun. Garnish with ketchup, mustard, tzatziki, cucumber, yogurt, etc. Enjoy.

COOKING NOTES:

Greek Chicken and Spaghetti

- ½ cup oregano
- ¾ cup crumbled Greek feta cheese
- ¾ cup tomato sauce
- ½ cup minced garlic
- 1 chicken cut into quarters
- 2 pounds Greek spaghetti #10

Preheat oven to 350 degrees.

Take each quarter of chicken and season it with the oregano, crumbled feta, tomato sauce, and garlic. Bake in the oven for about 30 minutes or until brown. Meanwhile, boil the spaghetti per the instructions, which are 8 to 10 minutes. Drain the spaghetti. Place chicken in a dish over the pasta and serve.

COOKING NOTES:

Name Day Bread (All Saints)

- ¾ cup sliced almonds
- 1 cup extra virgin olive oil
- 1/8 cup salt
- 1 1/8 package fast rising yeast
- 3¾ cups flour
- ¾ cup sugar
- ¾ cup cranberry juice
- ½ cup metaxa

Place all the ingredients in a mixing bowl and hand mix all ingredients together. Knead the dough very well. Place in at least a 10-inch round greased pan and bake at 375 degrees for 50 minutes or until brown.

COOKING NOTES:

Greek Fresh Orange Pie (Protokalatha Pie)

- 10 ounces yogurt
- ¾ cup freshly squeezed orange juice
- 3 cups vanilla ice cream
- ¾ cup warm water
- any kind of graham crackers for the crust
- ¼ cup sugar
- ¾ cup sliced almonds

Take the graham crackers and place along the bottom and the sides of a 9-inch pie pan. Place the water, yogurt, and freshly squeezed orange juice together in a mixing bowl. Add the ice cream, sugar and sliced almonds and mix. Place over the graham cracker crust pie pan. Freeze until it is hard.

COOKING NOTES:

Lamb Feta Pasta (Athenee Pastisto Pieto)

- 2½ cups crumbled Greek feta cheese
- ½ cup oregano
- pepper to taste
- 1 pound ground lamb
- 25 big pasta shells
- 24 ounces fresh-squeezed tomato juice
- ½ cup extra virgin olive oil

Put the pasta into a pan and boil for 7 minutes. Drain. Grease a casserole dish and place the pasta into the dish. Put the ground lamb, feta, tomato juice, oregano, pepper and extra virgin olive oil into the casserole dish and bake at 325 degrees for 55 minutes or until the lamb is brown. Enjoy!

COOKING NOTES:

Greek Popcorn

- 1 cup unpopped popcorn
- ½ cup shredded Greek feta cheese
- ½ cup shredded Greek kasseri cheese
- 1 tablespoon oregano
- 1 tablespoon basil
- ½ cup butter

Pop the popcorn in a hot air popper. Put ¼ of the popcorn in a large bowl. Sprinkle the feta, kasseri, oregano, basil and butter over the popcorn. Repeat for the remaining quarters. By seasoning every quarter at a time, it keeps the wonderful Greek seasoning taste through the whole batch of Greek popcorn.

COOKING NOTES:

Greek Corn Bread

- 1½ cups all-purpose flour
- 1½ cup cornmeal
- 1 teaspoon baking powder
- 2½ tablespoons sugar
- 1 teaspoon sea salt
- ¾ teaspoon baking soda
- 2 medium eggs
- ¼ cup basil leaves
- ¼ cup oregano
- 1 cup corn
- 6 tablespoons melted butter
- 1 cup kasseri cheese, shredded
- 1 cup eggnog

Preheat oven to 450 degrees. Mix the flour, cornmeal, sugar, baking powder, salt and baking soda in a mixing bowl. Mix very well. Make a small hole in the middle of the mixture but not all the way to the bottom of the bowl, about half the way down.

Mix the eggs, eggnog, corn, basil leaves, oregano, butter, and shredded kasseri together. Pour or spoon batter into a greased baking pan in a rectangle shape. Bake for 15 minutes or until brown on top. You may also put a toothpick in the center of the bread and when the toothpick comes out with no bread on it, the Greek corn bread is done. Let cool for 15 minutes or until you feel you can eat it. Some Greeks like to eat it hot!

COOKING NOTES:

Greek French Toast

- ½ cup shredded Greek feta cheese
- 8 eggs
- ¾ cup sugar
- 3 cups goat's milk
- 1 teaspoon liquid vanilla
- 1 Greek chocolate candy bar
- Pure Greek honey (melee)
- Greek bread loaf

Place all ingredients in a mixing bowl and mix together. Place 4 to 6 slices of Greek bread on a greased baking pan. Pour well mixed ingredients over each slice of bread. Bake at 350 degrees until golden brown on top. Pour Greek honey over the Greek French toast slices and enjoy. OPA!

COOKING NOTES:

Baked Greek Kasseri Cheese and Mushrooms

- 1 pound Greek kasseri cheese
- 1¼ tablespoons butter
- 3 tablespoons chopped walnuts
- 1¼ cup chopped fresh mushrooms
- 1¼ tablespoon Greek metaxa
- ½ teaspoon dill weed
- ½ teaspoon ground pepper

Begin by preheating your oven to 350 degrees. Mix the butter and walnuts in a mixing bowl. Put both in a small frying pan and let the butter melt. Mix while the butter is melting so it will not stick to the pan. Add the mushrooms, Greek metaxa, dill weed and pepper. Cook the mixture for 8 minutes on medium heat in a frying pan.

Cut the Greek kasseri cheese into quarters on a plate. Pour the cooked mixture over the kasseri. Let cool and serve. Yasoo!

COOKING NOTES:

Greek Fig Relish

- 4 figs, peeled
- ginger, just a pinch
- 1 cup chopped almonds
- ¼ cup extra virgin olive oil

Mix all the ingredients very, very, very well. Use as a topping for Greek bread or a relish for hors d'oeuvres or hamburgers and hot dogs.

COOKING NOTES:

Greek Tuna Steak

- 6 tuna steaks
- ¼ cup basil
- ¼ cup dill weed
- ¼ cup extra virgin olive oil
- 1 chopped tomato
- ½ cup minced garlic
- ¾ cup crumbled Greek feta cheese

Preheat oven to 350 degrees. Bake tuna for 7 minutes. Mix all other ingredients in a mixing bowl and put into a frying pan. Let simmer for 5 minutes on medium heat. Pour over the tuna steaks and bake for 30 minutes. Enjoy!

COOKING NOTES:

Greek Village Squid Salad
(Horiatiko Kalamari Salata)

- 3 sliced tomatoes
- 3 cups sliced onions
- ½ cup shredded Greek feta cheese
- ½ cup shredded Greek kasseri cheese
- ½ cup extra virgin olive oil
- ¼ cup Greek red wine
- ½ cup basil
- ½ cup dill weed

Mix all ingredients together except for the oil and the Greek wine. Pour the oil and the Greek wine over the entire salad and try to cover all the ingredients.

COOKING NOTES:

Greek Scrambled Eggs

- ½ cup Greek feta cheese
- ¼ cup oregano
- ¼ cup extra virgin olive oil
- 1 teaspoon salt
- 1 teaspoon pepper
- 3 large eggs
- 1/8 cup melted butter

Beat the eggs very, very well. Pour the other ingredients into the egg mixture. Place in a frying pan. Cook for a few minutes or until there is a yellow cooked appearance. Turn the scrambled eggs over and cook for two more minutes or until there is a yellow cooked appearance. Enjoy.

COOKING NOTES:

Greek Baked Cod

- ¼ cup extra virgin olive oil
- ¾ cup crumbled Greek feta cheese
- 4 tablespoon chopped oregano
- 4 tablespoon chopped basil
- 2 cloves minced garlic
- 1 tablespoon sea salt
- 1 tablespoon pepper
- 2 pounds cod fish
- ¼ cup freshly squeezed lemons

Preheat oven to 375 degrees. Mix all the ingredients together except the cod fish. Rinse the cod fish very, very, very well. Place cod fish in a baking pan. Pour lemon over the cod fish. Pour the mixed ingredients over the cod fish. Bake for about 30 minutes, or until it is opaque through the middle. Enjoy!

COOKING NOTES:

Gyro Sandwich

- 1½ pounds ground lamb
- ¼ cup minced garlic
- 1 tablespoon ground pepper
- ¼ cup oregano
- ¼ cup basil
- 1¼ teaspoon thyme
- 1½ tablespoons onion powder
- 1 teaspoon salt
- Greek bread

Preheat broiler or prepare barbeque. Combine ingredients lightly but thoroughly in large bowl. Shape into patties. Bake for 20 minutes on one side and 15 minutes on the other side. Place in Greek bread and enjoy with some yogurt or tzatziki.

COOKING NOTES:

Greek Yogurt Sauce

- 1 cup plain yogurt
- ¼ cup minced garlic
- ½ cup finely chopped cucumber
- salt
- pepper
- ¼ cup finely chopped onion
- ¼ cup extra virgin oil

Mix all the ingredients together well. Put in the refrigerator for 20 minutes. Use as a topping for beef, lamb, pork, fish, or use as an appetizer sauce for almost any item.

COOKING NOTES:

Greek Spanakopetes

- 1 cup Greek crumbled feta cheese
- 1 cup Greek kasseri cheese
- 2 cups chopped fresh spinach
- ¾ teaspoon pepper
- 1¼ teaspoon dried basil
- 1¼ teaspoon oregano
- 2 teaspoons dill weed
- 1 box Greek filo
- 2 eggs
- 1 cup butter

Preheat oven to 400 degrees. Mix all ingredients together in a bowl. Then beat the eggs in a separate bowl. Spread out the filo. Put filling in the center of each layer of filo. Brush outside of each with egg. Bake 15 minutes, lower heat to 300 degrees, and bake 15 more minutes.

COOKING NOTES:

Tyropita

- 1 cup butter
- 3 tablespoons extra virgin olive oil
- 1 box filo
- 4 eggs
- 4 tablespoons yogurt
- 1 cup crumbled Greek feta cheese
- 1 cup Greek kasseri

Preheat oven to 350 degrees. Mix the eggs and yogurt with the cheeses. In a greased baking pan, cover bottom of pan with 1 layer of dough. Brush with oil and butter. Put the next layer of filo on top of that. brush with oil mixture. Spread 1 to 2 tablespoons of filling. Repeat. Lower heat to 300 degrees. Bake 45 minutes or until well browned.

Make sure the bottom is browning as well. Set aside for 5-10 minutes under foil wrap. Serve.

COOKING NOTES:

Greek Halvah Chocolate

- 1 cup goat's milk
- 1 teaspoon vanilla
- 3/4 cup sesame seeds
- 1¾ cups brown sugar
- 1 cup Greek chocolate candy bar

Cook sugar and milk and chocolate candy bar in a sauce pot over medium heat of 230 degrees. Remove from fire and add sesame seeds and vanilla but do not mix in. Let it cool about 3 minutes. Mix with a spoon for a few seconds and pour quickly into a buttered pan.

COOKING NOTES:

Makaronia

- 1 package of Greek spaghetti #10
- ¾ pound sweet butter
- ½ pound shredded Greek feta
- ½ pound shredded kasseri
- 15 Greek kalamata olives, pitless and shaved

In a large saucepan melt the butter. Add the cheese and stir it in.

Add the pasta (which has been boiled for 8 minutes), and toss it in so that it is well coated with the butter and the cheeses. Add the shaved olives and toss them in as well.

COOKING NOTES:

INDEX

Printed in the United States
17577LVS00001B/280-303

9 781413 712070